W9-BSI-440

A Note to Parents

DK READERS is a compelling program for beginning readers, designed in conjunction with leading literacy experts, including Dr. Linda Gambrell, Distinguished Professor of Education at Clemson University. Dr. Gambrell has served as President of the National Reading Conference, the College Reading Association, and the International Reading Association.

Beautiful illustrations and superb full-color photographs combine with engaging, easy-to-read stories to offer a fresh approach to each subject in the series. Each DK READER is guaranteed to capture a child's interest while developing his or her reading skills, general knowledge, and love of reading.

The five levels of DK READERS are aimed at different reading abilities, enabling you to choose the books that are exactly right for your child:

Pre-level 1: Learning to read
Level 1: Beginning to read
Level 2: Beginning to read alone
Level 3: Reading alone
Level 4: Proficient readers

The "normal" age at which a child begins to read can be anywhere from three to eight years old. Adult participation through the lower levels is very helpful for providing encouragement, discussing storylines, and sounding out unfamiliar words.

No matter which level you select, you can be sure that you are helping your child learn to read, then read to learn!

DK

LONDON, NEW YORK, MUNICH,
MELBOURNE, and DELHI

Editor Emma Grange
Designers Jon Hall, Sandra Perry
Senior Pre-Production Producer Jennifer Murray
Producer Louise Minihane
Managing Editor Elizabeth Dowsett
Design Manager Ron Stobbart
Publishing Manager Julie Ferris
Art Director Lisa Lanzarini
Publishing Director Simon Beecroft

Reading Consultant
Linda B. Gambrell, Ph.D.

Dorling Kindersley would like to thank: Randi Sørensen and
Robert Stefan Ekblom at the LEGO Group and J. W. Rinzler,
Leland Chee, Troy Alders, and Carol Roeder at Lucasfilm.

First American Edition, 2014
10 9 8 7 6 5 4 3 2 1
Published in the United States by DK Publishing
4th Floor, 345 Hudson Street, New York, New York 10014

001–196543–July/14

Page design copyright © 2014 Dorling Kindersley Limited

LEGO, the LEGO logo, the Brick and Knob configurations,
and the Minifigure are trademarks of the LEGO Group.
© 2014 The LEGO Group
Produced by Dorling Kindersley Limited under license
from the LEGO Group.

© 2014 Lucasfilm Ltd. & ™. All rights reserved.
Used under authorization.

DK books are available at special discounts when purchased in bulk
for sales promotions, premiums, fund-raising, or educational use.
For details, contact: DK Publishing Special Markets, 4th Floor,
345 Hudson Street, New York, New York 10014
SpecialSales@dk.com

A catalog record for this book is available
from the Library of Congress.

ISBN: 978-1-4654-2031-2 (Paperback)
ISBN: 978-1-4654-2030-5 (Hardcover)

Color reproduction in the UK by Altaimage
Printed and bound in China

All other images © Dorling Kindersley
For further information see: www.dkimages.com

Discover more at
www.dk.com
www.starwars.com
www.LEGO.com/starwars

Contents

DK READERS

READING 3 ALONE

LEGO STAR WARS®

RETURN OF THE JEDI™

XZ
IR
G

Written by
Emma Grange

Mon Mothma

General Madine

Saving the galaxy

Here are some very brave rebels.
They are fighting to free the galaxy
from the control of the evil Empire.
They may not look like much, but
they have great courage and have
faced many battles without fear.

Rebel Pilot

Admiral
Ackbar

Rebel
Commando

After their last battle with the
Empire, the rebels were scattered
throughout the galaxy. Now they
are looking for a way to defeat
the Empire once and for all.

One of the rebel leaders, Mon
Mothma, is planning their next
move. Soon, she will summon all of
the rebel pilots, troopers, and fighters.

The ruler of the Empire is the sinister Sith Lord Darth Sidious, also known as the Emperor. He has an equally villainous apprentice named Darth Vader. The Sith seek power and control for themselves.

Red Guard

Darth
Sidious

Darth
Vader

The Emperor and his apprentice
have a vast army to serve them.
Look out for the Royal Red Guards
and the scary stormtroopers!

Darth Sidious thinks that it will
be easy to defeat the rebels. He has
a secret plan to make sure that the
Empire cannot be beaten…

Stormtroopers

Secret weapon

This moon-shaped object may look familiar. It is called the Death Star and it is the Empire's secret weapon. In fact, it is their second Death Star. The first Death Star was destroyed in an act of great daring by the rebels. This time, Darth Sidious and Darth Vader are taking no chances. The new Death Star is protected by an impenetrable, super-strong shield system, making it almost impossible to destroy.

The rebels will have to find a way to turn off the shield!

Vader's past

Before Darth Vader joined the Sith he was a Jedi named Anakin Skywalker. Anakin used the Force for good, in order to protect the galaxy. However, Darth Sidious persuaded him to join the dark side, promising him he would find greater power there.

Anakin
Skywalker

Jedi Knight
The Jedi also use the Force but, unlike the Sith, they use it for good and never for evil.

When Anakin became the Sith Lord Darth Vader, he didn't know he was leaving behind a son and a daughter. That son is the rebel Luke Skywalker, who is now training to be a Jedi Knight. Luke and Vader have fought once before. In order to defeat the rebels, Vader must either turn Luke to the dark side—or destroy him.

Darth Vader looks fierce and frightening. He has a dark and secret past.

Skywalker and friends

Luke Skywalker is determined to defeat the Sith and free the galaxy from the Empire. He also wants to save his father and bring him back to the light side of the Force.

First, he must rescue his friend Han Solo, who is being held prisoner on the planet Tatooine.

Princess
Leia

Luke
Skywalker

Han Solo has saved Luke's life more than once. Now Luke has a chance to save him in return!

For this mission, Luke is joined by a collection of Han's closest friends: the rebel Princess Leia, the Wookiee Chewbacca, the two droids R2-D2 and C-3PO, and Han's old friend Lando Calrissian.

C-3PO

R2-D2

Chewbacca

Lando Calrissian

Frozen solid

Han has been frozen in a material called carbonite to prevent him from escaping.

Jabba the Hutt

This slimy, green slug-like creature is crime lord Jabba the Hutt. Jabba has amassed great wealth and power on the planet Tatooine by stealing and smuggling. He employs many people to do his dirty work for him. He expects those people to always obey him. If they don't, then they had better watch out!

Han Solo used to work for Jabba, but he ended up owing him a lot of money. For revenge, Jabba plans to hold Han prisoner forever.

Many guards protect Jabba from all of his enemies and keep him safe in his palace.

Jabba's collection

Jabba loves collecting things, especially spice, money, and valuable objects. He owns a vast collection of droids. He also likes collecting people and keeping them as slaves.

At Jabba's command, some of his slaves must perform to entertain him. A girl named Oola dances, while a small, blue musician named Max Rebo plays music with a special instrument called a red ball organ.

The prize of Jabba's collection is a meat-eating monster called the rancor. Anyone who displeases Jabba is thrown down to the rancor pit.

Oola

red ball
organ

Max Rebo

Jabba's rancor lives in a pit beneath the
palace. On Jabba's instruction, a trapdoor
opens and people fall down below!

trapdoor

Tatooine mission

Han's friends have several sneaky plans to try to free him from the clutches of Jabba the Hutt.

First they send R2-D2 and C-3PO with a message. Luke offers the droids as a gift. Greedy Jabba takes the droids, but refuses to talk about releasing Han!

Then Princess Leia arrives disguised as a bounty hunter. In the middle of the night, Leia frees Han from the carbonite, but is soon discovered by Jabba. As punishment, Leia will become Jabba's slave.

Jabba's palace

Han is relieved to be freed from the carbonite. His imprisonment has made him feel weak and temporarily unable to fight!

Luke arrives to talk to Jabba face to face. His Jedi mind tricks only make Jabba laugh. When Luke tries to blast Jabba, he falls through the trapdoor into the rancor pit!

Bounty hunters
Bounty hunters work for the highest bidder, often capturing their prey for a large reward.

In the rancor pit

The hideous rancor was once given to Jabba as a birthday present. It has huge teeth and claws, and is kept in a pit beneath the palace.

When Luke falls into the rancor pit he must use all of his Jedi powers and some creativity to escape. Using a handy bone, he tricks the carnivorous creature and then manages to destroy it before he is eaten.

Not everybody is pleased that Luke has escaped the fearsome beast. Jabba is sad to have lost his pet, and now he must think of another way to rid himself of his unwelcome visitors.

Guard

Escaping the Sarlacc

Far out in the Tatooine desert, Jabba has something bigger and scarier waiting for Luke Skywalker and his friends.

The Sarlacc creature lives buried deep in the desert sands. Can you see its beak and tentacles above the sand? The Sarlacc is always hungry. Jabba plans to feed it his enemies as a small snack!

Lando Calrissian

Jabba's Desert Skiff

Unfortunately for Jabba, nothing goes according to plan. Luke attacks Jabba's guards with the lightsaber that R2-D2 had hidden, while Leia frees herself from Jabba. Lando and Han blow up Jabba's barge, and the lucky Sarlacc eats many of Jabba's guards. Delicious!

Guard

Lightsaber

Sarlacc

Grand Jedi Master

Reunited once more, the rebels are ready to face the Empire. However, Luke knows that he must complete his training with Jedi Master Yoda on the swampy planet Dagobah. Then he will truly be a Jedi.

Yoda is more than 900 years old
and has seen many battles. He is still
strong in the Force, but now he is old
and tired. He knows
that it is time to
leave this life and
become one with
the Force.

Jedi teacher
Yoda has watched
over Luke Skywalker
from afar for many
years. Now he knows
that the young Jedi is
ready to take on the
Sith by himself.

Long-lost sister

Luke is shocked to learn that he has a twin sister—his rebel friend Princess Leia!

The last Jedi?

After Yoda's death, Luke is visited by the Force ghost of his old friend Obi-Wan Kenobi. It was Obi-Wan who first told Luke he could be a Jedi, before he let himself be defeated by Darth Vader.

Obi-Wan has some last words of wisdom for Luke. He confirms that Darth Vader is Luke's father. Luke feels that Vader is not all evil.

He also warns Luke to be wary of the Emperor, who plans to lure him to the dark side. The temptation might be great. Beware the dark side, Luke!

Rebel attack

Back on board their Star Cruiser base, *Home One*, the rebels make plans to destroy the new Death Star.

Mon Mothma gives Han Solo a special mission to blow up the shield generator that is protecting the Death Star.

Admiral Ackbar

Mon Mothma

Hologram of the Death Star

The shield generator is on the forest moon of Endor and is guarded by Imperial forces. The rebels must sneak past the Empire's fierce stormtroopers and scout troopers to destroy the shield.

If they are discovered or defeated, their mission will be a failure!

Lando Calrissian

General Madine

On Endor

Scout trooper

Down on Endor's moon, the rebels soon run into trouble. Some scout troopers have wandered far from their base on a mission. They are not pleased to bump into the rebels!

Luckily for the rebels, the troopers are not very clever. As Luke and Leia chase after the scout troopers on their speeder bikes, one of them flies into a tree! Unfortunately, during the chase, Leia is separated from her friends.

Forest moon
This small moon is covered in lush forests. It orbits the planet Endor, and is usually a peaceful place.

Speeder bike

For now, Han and Luke must
continue without her.

Wicket

Ewok warrior

Chief Chirpa

Meeting the Ewoks

As the rebels travel further into the woods, they fall into an Ewok trap! Camouflaged among the trees on the forest moon, these small furry creatures are expert hunters.

The Ewoks plan on eating the rebels, but after some persuading, the rebels are freed and reunited with Leia—who has already made friends with one Ewok named Wicket.

Ewok leader
Chief Chirpa leads the Ewok tribe. He and the Ewoks decide to help the rebels.

Teebo

Logray

The curious Ewoks are not sure what to make of the rebels at first. The Ewoks could show them the way to the shield generator, but it would be safer to not get involved.

Eventually, the rebels, with help from C-3PO, persuade the Ewoks to help them and free their planet from the Empire forever.

Shield generator

The Ewoks lead the rebels to the shield generator. The shield protects the Empire's giant weapon and can be disabled only by blowing up the bunker and adjoining satellite dish.

Darth Sidious sends a small army of stormtroopers to surround the rebels.

The rebels have brought the droids R2-D2 and C-3PO along for this special task. However, it looks like Darth Sidious knew of the rebels' plans all along. It was all part of the Sith Lord's evil trap.

Droid friends

The loyal droid R2-D2 is programmed to work with computers. He could work faster if his friend C-3PO stopped bothering him!

The clever Ewoks use everything they have in the fight against the Empire.

Battle of Endor

The Ewoks may look cute, but they fight fiercely. When their planet is threatened, they do everything they can to help the rebels.

Some Ewoks gather sticks and stones to throw at the stormtroopers. Others operate catapults to launch large rocks at the approaching forces. Well done, Ewoks!

Now that the scout troopers and stormtroopers have all been vanquished, the droids can blow up the Death Star's shield generator. The rebels' grand plan is nearly complete.

Sith vs. Jedi

Luke has to confront Darth Sidious. He knows Sidious will try to persuade him to join the Sith, but Luke is ready to refuse him.

Darth Sidious is angered by Luke's refusal. The Jedi is no longer useful to him and so he blasts him with deadly Force lightning. Luke is no match for Darth Sidious's dark side powers.

Force lightning
The Force is a powerful energy. Darth Sidious uses it to create deadly Force lightning that can fatally harm his opponents.

Darth Vader is torn. He turned from the Jedi to become a Sith many years ago, but he cannot stand aside and watch his son be destroyed. Which side will he choose? Is there still some good left in Darth Vader?

Father and son

In the end, Darth Vader chooses love for his son over fear of his Sith Master. At great risk to himself, he grabs Darth Sidious and throws him down a deep reactor shaft. Darth Sidious is destroyed in a deadly explosion.

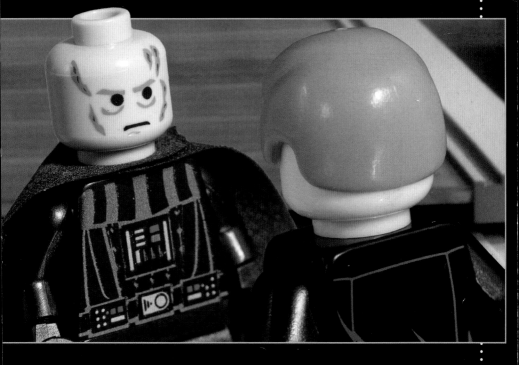

Darth Vader has saved Luke and destroyed the Emperor. These selfless actions finally free him from the dark side of the Force, but at a great cost. He has been fatally injured by the Emperor's Force lightning.

X-wing Fighter

Final act

Meanwhile, Lando Calrissian is leading an air attack in space against the Empire from onboard Han Solo's ship, the *Millennium Falcon*. Imperial pilots fly after him in their TIE fighters, but they are not fast enough to catch Lando or the rebel pilots in their X-wing starfighters.

Millennium Falcon

With the shield down, Lando is able to fly right into the very center of the Death Star's core. From the inside he then causes an explosion that blows it into thousands of tiny pieces. Lando and Luke flee to safety just in time!

Galaxy celebrations

The galaxy is free at last from the control of the Empire! The menace of the Sith has also been destroyed.

People from different planets across the galaxy celebrate the good news. The combined courage of the rebels, Jedi, droids, and some small Ewoks helped to save the galaxy.

Luke is glad to be reunited with Han and his sister, Leia. He knows that he could not have done anything without them, and the help of Jedi Masters Obi-Wan Kenobi and Yoda.

The galaxy is peaceful once more, but who knows what challenges the future holds?

Glossary

Adjoining
Next to or connected to.

Amassed
Gained or collected many things.

Apprentice
Student or pupil.

Bunker
Strong building, used to keep things safe.

Camouflaged
Disguised to resemble and blend in with the surroundings.

Carnivorous
Creature that eats an entirely meat-based diet.

Confront
Question or challenge.

Droid
Metal robot.

Empire
Group of nations ruled over by one leader, who is called an Emperor.

Galaxy
Group of millions of stars and planets.

Generator
Machine that creates power, usually electrical.

Hologram
3-D image of someone or something that is not there, used as a way to communicate.

Impenetrable
Impossible to pass through or enter.

Imperial
Belonging to the Empire.

Jedi
Someone who uses the Force to protect people and keep the peace.

Lightsaber
A weapon made of pure Force energy, used like a sword.

Lure
Persuade someone to go somewhere or do something with the promise of a reward.

Menace
A threat. Something likely to cause danger.

Rebel
Person who rises up to fight against the current ruler.

Scout
Soldier sent on ahead to check for signs of the enemy and report back.

Selfless
Unselfish, to think of and act for others before oneself.

Sinister
Frightening, evil.

Sith
Someone who uses the Force for selfish reasons and to gain power.

Skiff
Shallow, flat-bottomed vehicle.

Smuggling
Illegally moving valuable goods from one place to another and selling them for a profit.

Snare
Catch someone inside a trap.

Summon
Gather or call a group of people together.

Temptation
Feeling of wanting to do something that sounds attractive.

TIE Fighter
Type of starfighter flown by the Empire's forces.

Vanquished
Utterly defeated.

X-wing
Type of starfighter flown by rebel forces.

Index

The Twits

KNOPF BOOKS BY ROALD DAHL

Charlie and the Chocolate Factory

Charlie and the Great Glass Elevator

Danny the Champion of the World

The Enormous Crocodile

Fantastic Mr. Fox

George's Marvelous Medicine

James and the Giant Peach

The Mildenhall Treasure

Roald Dahl's Revolting Rhymes

The Wonderful Story of Henry Sugar and Six More

ROALD DAHL

The Twits

Illustrated by Quentin Blake

ALFRED A. KNOPF
New York

THIS IS A BORZOI BOOK PUBLISHED BY ALFRED A. KNOPF

Text copyright © 1980 by Roald Dahl Nominee Limited
Illustrations copyright © 1980 by Quentin Blake
Jacket illustration copyright © 1996 by Quentin Blake
All rights reserved under International and Pan-American Copyright Conventions.
Published in the United States of America by Alfred A. Knopf,
an imprint of Random House Children's Books, a division of
Random House, Inc., New York, and simultaneously in Canada by
Random House of Canada Limited, Toronto.
Distributed by Random House, Inc., New York.
Originally published in Great Britain by Jonathan Cape Ltd. and
in the United States by Alfred A. Knopf, a division of Random House, Inc., in 1980.

www.randomhouse.com/kids

KNOPF, BORZOI BOOKS, and the colophon are registered trademarks of Random House, Inc.

Library of Congress Cataloging-in-Publication Data
Dahl, Roald.
The Twits / Roald Dahl ; illustrated by Quentin Blake.
p. cm.
Summary: The misadventures of two terrible old people who enjoy playing nasty tricks
and are finally outwitted by a family of monkeys.
[1. Humorous stories.] I. Blake, Quentin, ill. II. Title.
PZ7.D1515 Tw 2002
[Fic]—dc21
2002066074

ISBN 0-375-82242-9 (trade)
ISBN 0-375-92242-3 (lib. bdg.)

Printed in the United States of America

September 2002

10 9 8 7 6 5 4 3 2

Revised Edition

For Emma

CONTENTS

Hairy Faces

What a lot of hairy-faced men there are around nowadays.

When a man grows hair all over his face it is impossible to tell what he really looks like.

Perhaps that's why he does it. He'd rather you didn't know.

Then there's the problem of washing.

When the very hairy ones wash their faces, it must be as big a job as when you and I wash the hair on our heads.

So what I want to know is this. How often do all these hairy-faced men wash their faces? Is it only once a week, like us, on Sunday nights? And do they shampoo it? Do they use a hairdryer? Do they rub hair tonic in to stop their faces from going bald? Do they go to a barber to have their hairy faces cut and trimmed or do they do it themselves in front of the bathroom mirror with nail scissors?

I don't know. But next time you see a man with a hairy face (which will probably be as soon as you step out onto the street) maybe you will look at him more closely and start wondering about some of these things.

Mr. Twit

Mr. Twit was one of these very hairy-faced men. The whole of his face except for his forehead, his eyes and his nose, was covered with thick hair. The stuff even sprouted in revolting tufts out of his nostrils and ear-holes.

Mr. Twit felt that this hairiness made him look terrifically wise and grand. But in truth he was neither of these things. Mr. Twit was a twit. He was born a twit. And now at the age of sixty, he was a bigger twit than ever.

The hair on Mr. Twit's face didn't grow smooth and matted as it does on most hairy-faced men. It grew in spikes that stuck out straight like the bristles of a nailbrush.

And how often did Mr. Twit wash this bristly nailbrushy face of his?

The answer is NEVER, not even on Sundays.

He hadn't washed it for years.

Dirty Beards

As you know, an ordinary unhairy face like yours or mine simply gets a bit smudgy if it is not washed often enough, and there's nothing so awful about that.

But a hairy face is a very different matter. Things *cling* to hairs, especially food. Things like gravy go right in among the hairs and stay there. You and I can wipe our smooth faces with a washcloth and we quickly look more or less all right again, but the hairy man cannot do that.

We can also, if we are careful, eat our meals without spreading food all over our faces. But not so the hairy man. Watch carefully next time you see a hairy man eating his lunch and you will notice that even if he opens his mouth very wide, it is impossible for him to get a spoonful of beef stew or ice cream and chocolate sauce into it without leaving some of it on the hairs.

Mr. Twit didn't even bother to open his mouth wide when he ate. As a result (and because he never washed) there were always hundreds of bits of old breakfasts and lunches and suppers sticking to the hairs around his face. They weren't big bits, mind you, because he used to wipe those off with the back of his hand or on his sleeve while he was eating. But if you looked closely (not that you'd ever want to) you would see tiny little specks of dried-up scrambled eggs stuck to the hairs, and spinach and tomato ketchup and fishsticks and minced chicken livers and all the other disgusting things Mr. Twit liked to eat.

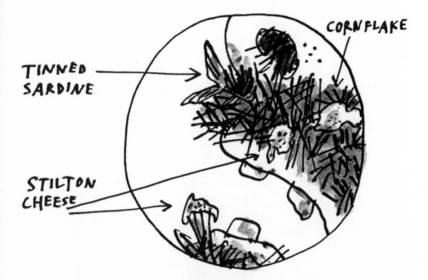

TINNED SARDINE

CORNFLAKE

STILTON CHEESE

If you looked closer still (hold your noses, ladies and gentlemen), if you peered deep into the moustachy bristles sticking out over his upper lip, you would probably see much larger objects that had escaped the wipe of his hand, things that had been there for months and months, like a piece of maggoty green cheese or a moldy old cornflake or even the slimy tail of a tinned sardine.

Because of all this, Mr. Twit never went really hungry. By sticking out his tongue and curling it sideways to explore the hairy jungle around his mouth, he was always able to find a tasty morsel here and there to nibble on.

What I am trying to tell you is that Mr. Twit was a foul and smelly old man.

He was also an extremely horrid old man as you will find out in a moment.

Mrs. Twit

Mrs. Twit was no better than her husband.

She did not, of course, have a hairy face. It was a pity she didn't because that, at any rate, would have hidden some of her fearful ugliness.

Take a look at her.

Have you ever seen a woman with an uglier face than that? I doubt it.

But the funny thing is that Mrs. Twit wasn't born ugly. She'd had quite a nice face when she was young. The ugliness had grown upon her year by year as she got older.

Why would that happen? I'll tell you why.

If a person has ugly thoughts, it begins to show on the face. And when that person has ugly thoughts every day, every week, every year, the face gets uglier and uglier until it gets so ugly you can hardly bear to look at it.

A person who has good thoughts cannot ever be ugly. You can have a wonky nose and a crooked mouth and a double chin and stick-out teeth, but if you have good thoughts they will shine out of your face like sunbeams and you will always look lovely.

Nothing good shone out of Mrs. Twit's face.

In her right hand she carried a walking stick. She used to tell people that this was because she had warts growing on the sole of her left foot and walking was painful. But the real reason she carried a stick was so that she could hit things with it, things like dogs and cats and small children.

And then there was the glass eye. Mrs. Twit had a glass eye that was always looking the other way.

The Glass Eye

You can play a lot of tricks with a glass eye because you can take it out and pop it back in again any time you like. You can bet your life Mrs. Twit knew all the tricks.

One morning she took out her glass eye and dropped it into Mr. Twit's mug of beer when he wasn't looking.

Mr. Twit sat there drinking the beer slowly. The froth made a white ring on the hairs around his mouth. He wiped the white froth on to his sleeve and wiped his sleeve on his trousers.

"You're plotting something," Mrs. Twit said, keeping her back turned so he wouldn't see that she had taken out her glass eye. "Whenever you go all quiet like that I know very well you're plotting something."

Mrs. Twit was right. Mr. Twit was plotting away like mad. He was trying to think up a really nasty trick he could play on his wife that day.

"You'd better be careful," Mrs. Twit said, "because when I see you starting to plot, I watch you like a wombat."

"Oh, do shut up, you old hag," Mr. Twit said. He went on drinking his beer, and his evil mind kept working away on the latest horrid trick he was going to play on the old woman.

Suddenly, as Mr. Twit tipped the last drop of beer down his throat, he caught sight of Mrs. Twit's awful glass eye staring up at him from the bottom of the mug. It made him jump.

"I told you I was watching you," cackled Mrs. Twit. "I've got eyes everywhere so you'd better be careful."

The Frog

To pay her back for the glass eye in his beer, Mr. Twit decided he would put a frog in Mrs. Twit's bed.

He caught a big one down by the pond and carried it back secretly in a box.

That night, when Mrs. Twit was in the bathroom getting ready for bed, Mr. Twit slipped the frog between her sheets. Then he got into his own bed and waited for the fun to begin.

Mrs. Twit came back and climbed into her bed and put out the light. She lay there in the dark scratching her tummy. Her tummy was itching. Dirty old hags like her always have itchy tummies.

Then all at once she felt something cold and slimy crawling over her feet. She screamed.

"What's the matter with you?" Mr. Twit said.

"Help!" screamed Mrs. Twit, bouncing about. "There's something in my bed!"

"I'll bet it's that Giant Skillywiggler I saw on the floor just now," Mr. Twit said.

"That *what?*" screamed Mrs. Twit.

"I tried to kill it but it got away," Mr. Twit said. "It's got teeth like screwdrivers!"

"Help!" screamed Mrs. Twit. "Save me! It's all over my feet!"

"It'll bite off your toes," said Mr. Twit.

Mrs. Twit fainted.

Mr. Twit got out of bed and fetched a jug of cold water. He poured the water over Mrs. Twit's head to revive her. The frog crawled up from under the sheets to get near the water. It started jumping about on the pillow. Frogs love water. This one was having a good time.

When Mrs. Twit came to, the frog had just jumped onto her face. This is not a nice thing to happen to anyone in bed at night. She screamed again.

"By golly it *is* a Giant Skillywiggler!" Mr. Twit said. "It'll bite off your nose."

Mrs. Twit leapt out of bed and flew downstairs and spent the night on the sofa. The frog went to sleep on her pillow.

The Wormy Spaghetti

The next day, to pay Mr. Twit back for the frog trick, Mrs. Twit sneaked out into the garden and dug up some worms. She chose big long ones and put them in a tin and carried the tin back to the house under her apron.

At one o'clock, she cooked spaghetti for lunch and she mixed the worms in with the spaghetti, but only on her husband's plate. The worms didn't show because everything was covered with tomato sauce and sprinkled with cheese.

"Hey, my spaghetti's moving!" cried Mr. Twit, poking around in it with his fork.

"It's a new kind," Mrs. Twit said, taking a mouthful from her own plate which of course had no

worms. "It's called Squiggly Spaghetti. It's delicious.
Eat it up while it's nice and hot."

Mr. Twit started eating, twisting the long
tomato-covered strings around his fork and shovel-
ing them into his mouth. Soon there was tomato
sauce all over his hairy chin.

"It's not as good as the ordinary kind," he said,
talking with his mouth full. "It's too squishy."

"I find it very tasty," Mrs. Twit said. She was
watching him from the other end of the table. It gave
her great pleasure to watch him eating worms.

"I find it rather bitter," Mr. Twit said. "It's got a
distinctly bitter flavor. Buy the other kind next
time."

Mrs. Twit waited until Mr. Twit had eaten the
whole plateful. Then she said, "You want to know
why your spaghetti was squishy?"

Mr. Twit wiped the tomato sauce from his beard with a corner of the tablecloth. "Why?" he said.

"And why it had a nasty bitter taste?"

"Why?" he said.

"Because it was *worms!*" cried Mrs. Twit, clapping her hands and stamping her feet on the floor and rocking with horrible laughter.

The Funny Walking Stick

To pay Mrs. Twit back for the worms in his spaghetti, Mr. Twit thought up a really clever nasty trick.

One night, when the old woman was asleep, he crept out of bed and took her walking stick downstairs to his workshed. There he stuck a tiny round piece of wood (no thicker than a penny) onto the bottom of the stick.

This made the stick longer, but the difference was so small, the next morning Mrs. Twit didn't notice it.

The following night, Mr. Twit stuck on another tiny bit of wood. Every night, he crept downstairs and added an extra tiny thickness of wood to the end of the walking stick. He did it very neatly so that the extra bits looked like a part of the old stick.

Gradually, but oh so gradually, Mrs. Twit's walking stick was getting longer and longer.

Now when something is growing very very slowly, it is almost impossible to notice it happening. You yourself, for example, are actually growing taller every day that goes by, but you wouldn't think it, would you? It's happening so slowly you can't even notice it from one week to the next.

It was the same with Mrs. Twit's walking stick. It was all so slow and gradual that she didn't notice how long it was getting even when it was halfway up to her shoulder.

"That stick's too long for you," Mr. Twit said to her one day.

"Why so it is!" Mrs. Twit said, looking at the stick. "I've had a feeling there was something wrong but I couldn't for the life of me think what it was."

"There's something wrong all right," Mr. Twit said, beginning to enjoy himself.

"What *can* have happened?" Mrs. Twit said, staring at her old walking stick. "It must suddenly have grown longer."

"Don't be a fool!" Mr. Twit said. "How can a walking stick possibly grow longer? It's made of dead wood, isn't it? Dead wood can't grow."

"Then what on earth has happened?" cried Mrs. Twit.

"It's not the stick, it's *you!*" said Mr. Twit, grinning horribly. "It's *you* that's getting *shorter!* I've been noticing it for some time now."

"That's not true!" cried Mrs. Twit.

"You're shrinking, woman!" said Mr. Twit.

"It's not possible!"

"Oh yes it jolly well is," said Mr. Twit. "You're shrinking fast! You're shrinking *dangerously* fast! Why, you must have shrunk at least a foot in the last few days!"

"Never!" she cried.

"Of course you have! Take a look at your stick, you old goat, and see how much you've shrunk in comparison! You've got the *shrinks*, that's what you've got! You've got the dreaded *shrinks!*"

Mrs. Twit began to feel so trembly she had to sit down.

Mrs. Twit Has the Shrinks

As soon as Mrs. Twit sat down, Mr. Twit pointed at her and shouted, "There you are! You're sitting in your old chair and you've shrunk so much your feet aren't even touching the ground!"

Mrs. Twit looked down at her feet and by golly the man was right. Her feet were not touching the ground.

Mr. Twit, you see, had been just as clever with the chair as he'd been with the walking stick. Every night when he had gone downstairs and stuck a little bit extra onto the stick, he had done the same to the four legs of Mrs. Twit's chair.

"Just look at you sitting there in your same old chair," he cried, "and you've shrunk so much your feet are dangling in the air!"

Mrs. Twit went white with fear.

"You've got the *shrinks!*" cried Mr. Twit, pointing his finger at her like a pistol. "You've got them badly! You've got the most terrible case of shrinks I've ever seen!"

Mrs. Twit became so frightened she began to dribble. But Mr. Twit, still remembering the worms in his spaghetti, didn't feel sorry for her at all. "I suppose you know what *happens* to you when you get the shrinks?" he said.

"What?" gasped Mrs. Twit. "What happens?"

"Your head SHRINKS into your neck . . .

"And your neck SHRINKS into your body . . .

"And your body SHRINKS into your legs . . .

"And your legs SHRINK into your feet. And in the end there's nothing left except a pair of shoes and a bundle of old clothes."

"I can't bear it!" cried Mrs. Twit.

"It's a terrible disease," said Mr. Twit. "The worst in the world."

"How long have I got?" cried Mrs. Twit. "How long before I finish up as a bundle of old clothes and a pair of shoes?"

Mr. Twit put on a very solemn face. "At the rate you're going," he said, shaking his head sadly, "I'd say not more than ten or eleven days."

"But isn't there *anything* we can do?" cried Mrs. Twit.

"There's only one cure for the shrinks," said Mr. Twit.

"Tell me!" she cried. "Oh, tell me quickly!"

"We'll have to hurry!" said Mr. Twit.

"I'm ready. I'll hurry! I'll do anything you say!" cried Mrs. Twit.

"You won't last long if you don't," said Mr. Twit, giving her another grizzly grin.

"What is it I must do?" cried Mrs. Twit, clutching her cheeks.

"You've got to be *stretched*," said Mr. Twit.

Mrs. Twit Gets a Stretching

Mr. Twit led Mrs. Twit outdoors where he had everything ready for the great stretching.

He had one hundred balloons and lots of string.

He had a gas cylinder for filling the balloons.

He had fixed an iron ring into the ground.

"Stand here," he said, pointing to the iron ring. He then tied Mrs. Twit's ankles to the iron ring.

When that was done, he began filling the balloons with gas. Each balloon was on a long string and when it was filled with gas it pulled on its string, trying to go up and up. Mr. Twit tied the ends of the strings to the top half of Mrs. Twit's body. Some he tied around her neck, some under her arms, some to her wrists and some even to her hair.

Soon there were fifty colored balloons floating in the air above Mrs. Twit's head.

"Can you feel them stretching you?" asked Mr. Twit.

"I can! I can!" cried Mrs. Twit. "They're stretching me like mad."

He put on another ten balloons. The upward pull became very strong.

Mrs. Twit was quite helpless now. With her feet tied to the ground and her arms pulled upward by the balloons, she was unable to move. She was a prisoner, and Mr. Twit had intended to go away and leave her like that for a couple of days and nights to teach her a lesson. In fact, he was just about to leave when Mrs. Twit opened her big mouth and said something silly.

"Are you sure my feet are tied properly to the ground?" she gasped. "If those strings around my ankles break, it'll be goodbye for me!"

And that's what gave Mr. Twit his second nasty idea.

Mrs. Twit Goes Ballooning Up

"There's enough pull here to take me to the moon!" Mrs. Twit cried out.

"To take you to *the moon!*" exclaimed Mr. Twit. "What a ghastly thought! We wouldn't want anything like that to happen, oh dear me no!"

"We most certainly wouldn't!" cried Mrs. Twit. "Put some more string around my ankles quickly! I want to feel absolutely safe!"

"Very well, my angel," said Mr. Twit, and with a ghoulish grin on his lips he knelt down at her feet. He took a knife from his pocket and with one quick slash he cut through the strings holding Mrs. Twit's ankles to the iron ring.

She went up like a rocket.

"Help!" she screamed. "Save me!"

But there was no saving her now. In a few seconds she was high up in the blue blue sky and climbing fast.

Mr. Twit stood below looking up. "*What* a pretty sight!" he said to himself. "How lovely all those balloons look in the sky! And what a marvelous bit of luck for me! At last the old hag is lost and gone forever."

Mrs. Twit Goes Ballooning Down

Mrs. Twit may have been ugly and she may have been beastly, but she was not stupid.

High up there in the sky, she had a bright idea. "If I can get rid of some of these balloons," she said to herself, "I will stop going up and start to come down."

She began biting through the strings that held the balloons to her wrists and arms and neck and hair. Each time she bit through a string and let the balloon float away, the upward pull got less and her rate of climb slowed down.

When she had bitten through twenty strings, she stopped going up altogether. She stayed still in the air.

She bit through one more string.

Very very slowly, she began to float downward.

It was a calm day. There was no wind at all. And because of this, Mrs. Twit had gone absolutely straight up. She now began to come absolutely straight down.

As she floated gently down, Mrs. Twit's petticoat billowed out like a parachute, showing her long knickers. It was a grand sight on a glorious day, and thousands of birds came flying in from miles around to stare at this extraordinary old woman in the sky.

Mr. Twit Gets a Horrid Shock

Mr. Twit, who thought he had seen his ugly wife for the last time, was sitting in the garden celebrating with a mug of beer.

Silently, Mrs. Twit came floating down. When she was about the height of the house above Mr. Twit, she suddenly called out at the top of her voice, "Here I come, you grizzly old grunion! You rotten old turnip! You filthy old frumpet!"

Mr. Twit jumped as though he'd been stung by a giant wasp. He dropped his beer. He looked up. He gaped. He gasped. He gurgled. A few choking sounds came out of his mouth. "*Ughhhhhhhh!*" he said. "*Arghhhhhhhh! Ouchhhhhhhh!*"

"I'll get you for this!" shouted Mrs. Twit. She was floating down right on top of him. She was purple with rage and slashing the air with her long walking stick which she had somehow managed to hang on to all the time. "I'll swish you to a swazzle!" she shouted. "I'll swash you to a swizzle! I'll gnash you to a gnozzle! I'll gnosh you to a gnazzle!" And before Mr. Twit had time to run away, this bundle of balloons and petticoats and fiery fury landed right on top of him, lashing out with the stick and cracking him all over his body.

The House, the Tree, & the Monkey Cage

But that's enough of that. We can't go on forever watching these two disgusting people doing disgusting things to each other. We must get ahead with the story.

Here is a picture of Mr. and Mrs. Twit's house and garden. Some house! It looks like a prison. And not a window anywhere.

"Who wants windows?" Mr. Twit had said when they were building it. "Who wants every Tom, Dick and Harry peeping in to see what you're doing?" It didn't occur to Mr. Twit that windows were meant mainly for looking out of, not for looking into.

And what do you think of that ghastly garden?

Mrs. Twit was the gardener. She was very good at growing thistles and stinging-nettles. "I always grow plenty of spiky thistles and plenty of stinging-nettles," she used to say. "They keep out nasty nosy little children."

Near the house you can see Mr. Twit's workshed.

To one side there is The Big Dead Tree. It never has any leaves on it because it's dead.

And not far from the tree, you can see the monkey cage. There are four monkeys in it. They belong to Mr. Twit. You will hear about them later.

Hugtight Sticky Glue

Once a week, on Wednesdays, the Twits had Bird Pie
for supper. Mr. Twit caught the birds and Mrs. Twit
cooked them.

Mr. Twit was good at catching birds. On the day
before Bird Pie day, he would put the ladder up
against The Big Dead Tree and climb into the
branches with a bucket of glue and a paintbrush.
The glue he used was something called HUGTIGHT
and it was stickier than any other glue in the world.
He would paint it along the tops of all the branches
and then go away.

As the sun went down, birds would fly in from all
around to roost for the night in The Big Dead Tree.
They didn't know, poor things, that the branches

were all smeared with horrible HUGTIGHT. The moment they landed on a branch, their feet stuck and that was that.

The next morning, which was Bird Pie day, Mr. Twit would climb up the ladder again and grab all the wretched birds that were stuck to the tree. It didn't matter what kind they were—song thrushes, blackbirds, sparrows, crows, little jenny wrens, robins, anything—they all went into the pot for Wednesday's Bird Pie supper.

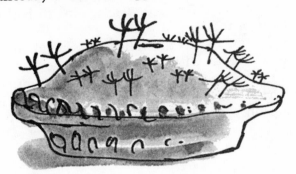

Four Sticky Little Boys

On one Tuesday evening after Mr. Twit had been up the ladder and smeared the tree with HUGTIGHT, four little boys crept into the garden to look at the monkeys. They didn't care about the thistles and stinging-nettles, not when there were monkeys to look at. After a while, they got tired of looking at the monkeys, so they explored further into the garden and found the ladder leaning against The Big Dead Tree. They decided to climb it just for fun.

There's nothing wrong with that.

The next morning, when Mr. Twit went out to collect the birds, he found four miserable little boys sitting in the tree, stuck as tight as could be by the seats of their pants to the branches. There were no birds because the presence of the boys had scared them away.

Mr. Twit was furious. "As there are no birds for my pie tonight," he shouted, "then it'll have to be *boys* instead!" He started to climb the ladder. "Boy Pie might be better than Bird Pie," he went on, grinning horribly. "More meat and not so many tiny little bones!"

The boys were terrified. "He's going to boil us!" cried one of them.

"He'll stew us alive!" wailed the second one.

"He'll cook us with carrots!" cried the third.

But the fourth little boy, who had more sense than the others, whispered, "Listen, I've just had an idea. We are only stuck by *the seats of our pants.* So

quick! Unbutton your pants and slip out of them and fall to the ground."

Mr. Twit had reached the top of the ladder and was just about to make a grab for the nearest boy when they all suddenly tumbled out of the tree and ran for home with their naked bottoms winking at the sun.

The Great Upside-Down Monkey Circus

Now for the monkeys.

The four monkeys in the cage in the garden were all one family. They were Muggle-Wump and his wife and their two small children.

But what on earth were Mr. and Mrs. Twit doing with monkeys in their garden?

Well, in the old days, they had both worked in a circus as monkey trainers. They used to teach monkeys to do tricks and to dress up in human clothes and to smoke pipes and all the rest of that nonsense.

Today, although they were retired, Mr. Twit still wanted to train monkeys. It was his dream that one day he would own the first GREAT UPSIDE-DOWN MONKEY CIRCUS in the world.

That meant that the monkeys had to do every-thing upside down. They had to dance upside down (on their hands with their feet in the air). They had to play football upside down. They had to balance one on top of the other upside down, with Muggle-Wump at the bottom and the smallest baby monkey at the very top. They even had to eat and drink upside down and that is not an easy thing to do because the food and water has to go *up* your throat instead of down it. In fact, it is almost impossible, but the monkeys simply had to do it otherwise they got nothing.

All this sounds pretty silly to you and me. It sounded pretty silly to the monkeys, too. They absolutely hated having to do this upside-down nonsense day after day. It made them giddy standing on their heads for hours on end. Sometimes the two small monkey children would faint with so much blood going to their heads. But Mr. Twit didn't care about that. He kept them practicing for six hours every day and if they didn't do as they were told, Mrs. Twit would soon come running with her beastly stick.

The Roly-Poly Bird to the Rescue

Muggle-Wump and his family longed to escape from the cage in Mr. Twit's garden and go back to the African jungle where they came from.

They hated Mr. and Mrs. Twit for making their lives so miserable.

They also hated them for what they did to the birds every Tuesday and Wednesday. "Fly away, birds!" they used to shout, jumping about in the cage and waving their arms. "Don't sit on that Big Dead Tree! It's just been smeared all over with sticky glue! Go and sit somewhere else!"

But these were English birds and they couldn't understand the weird African language the monkeys spoke. So they took no notice and went on using The Big Dead Tree and getting caught for Mrs. Twit's Bird Pie.

Then one day, a truly magnificent bird flew down out of the sky and landed on the monkey cage.

"Good heavens!" cried all the monkeys together. "It's the Roly-Poly Bird! What on earth are you doing over here in England, Roly-Poly Bird?" Like the monkeys, the Roly-Poly Bird came from Africa and he spoke the same language as they did.

"I've come for a holiday," said the Roly-Poly Bird. "I like to travel." He fluffed his marvelous colored feathers and looked down rather grandly at the monkeys. "For most people," he went on, "flying away on holiday is very expensive, but I can fly anywhere in the world for nothing."

"Do you know how to talk to these English birds?" Muggle-Wump asked him.

"Of course I do," said the Roly-Poly Bird. "It's no good going to a country and not knowing the language."

"Then we must hurry," said Muggle-Wump. "Today is Tuesday and over there you can already see the revolting Mr. Twit up the ladder painting sticky glue on all the branches of The Big Dead Tree. This evening when the birds come in to roost, you must warn them not to perch on that tree or they will be made into Bird Pie."

That evening, the Roly-Poly Bird flew around and around The Big Dead Tree singing out,

"There's sticky stick stuff all over the tree!
If you land in the branches, you'll never get free!
So fly away! Fly away! Stay up high!
Or you'll finish up tomorrow in a hot Bird Pie!"

No Bird Pie for Mr. Twit

The next morning when Mr. Twit came out with his huge basket to snatch all the birds from The Big Dead Tree, there wasn't a single one on it. They were all sitting on top of the monkey cage. The Roly-Poly Bird was there as well, and Muggle-Wump and his family were inside the cage and the whole lot of them were laughing at Mr. Twit.

Still No Bird Pie for Mr. Twit

Mr. Twit wasn't going to wait another week for his Bird Pie supper. He loved Bird Pie. It was his favorite meal. So that very same day, he went after the birds again. This time he smeared all the top bars of the monkey cage with sticky glue, as well as the branches of   The Big Dead Tree. "Now I'll get you," he said, "whichever one you sit on!"

The monkeys crouched inside the cage watching all this, and later on, when the Roly-Poly Bird came swooping in for an evening chat, they shouted out,

"Don't land on our cage, Roly-Poly Bird! It's covered with sticky glue! So is the tree!"

And that evening, as the sun went down and all the birds came in again to roost, the Roly-Poly Bird flew around and around the monkey cage and The Big Dead Tree, singing out his warning,

"There's sticky stuff now on the cage and the tree!
If you land on either, you'll never get free!
So fly away! Fly away! Stay up high!
Or you'll finish up tomorrow in a hot Bird Pie!"

Mr. & Mrs. Twit Go Off to Buy Guns

The next morning when Mr. Twit came out with his huge basket, not a single bird was sitting on either the monkey cage or The Big Dead Tree. They were all perched happily on the roof of Mr. Twit's house. The Roly-Poly Bird was up there as well, and the monkeys were in the cage and the whole lot of them were hooting with laughter at Mr. Twit.

"I'll wipe that silly laugh off your beaks!" Mr. Twit screamed at the birds. "I'll get you next time, you filthy feathery frumps! I'll wring your necks, the whole lot of you, and have you bubbling in the pot for Bird Pie before this day is out!"

"How are you going to do that?" asked Mrs. Twit, who had come outside to see what all the noise was about. "I won't have you smearing sticky glue all over the roof of our house!"

Mr. Twit went very close to Mrs. Twit and lowered his voice so that neither the birds nor monkeys should hear. "I've got a great idea," he said. "We'll both go into town right away and we'll buy a gun each! How's that?"

"Brilliant!" cried Mrs. Twit, grinning and showing her long yellow teeth. "We'll buy those big shotguns that spray out fifty bullets or more with each bang!"

"Exactly," said Mr. Twit. "Lock up the house while I go and make sure the monkeys are safely shut away."

Mr. Twit went over to the monkey cage. "Attention!" he barked in his fearsome monkey-trainer's voice. "Upside down all of you and jump to it! One on top of the other! Quick! Get on with it or you'll feel Mrs. Twit's stick across your backsides!"

Obediently, the poor monkeys stood on their hands and clambered one on top of the other, with Muggle-Wump at the bottom and the smallest child at the very top.

"Now stay there till we come back!" Mr. Twit ordered. "Don't you dare to move! And don't over-balance! When we return in two or three hours time, I shall expect to find you all in exactly the same position as you are now! You understand?"

With that, Mr. Twit marched away. Mrs. Twit went with him. And the monkeys were left alone with the birds.

Muggle-Wump Has an Idea

As soon as Mr. and Mrs. Twit had disappeared down the road, the monkeys all flipped back onto their feet the right way up. "Quick, get the key!" Muggle-Wump called out to the Roly-Poly Bird who was still sitting on the roof of the house.

"What key?" shouted the Roly-Poly Bird.

"The key to the door of our cage," cried Muggle-Wump. "It's hanging on a nail in the workshed. That's where he always puts it."

The Roly-Poly Bird flew down and came back with the key in his beak. Muggle-Wump reached a hand through the bars of the cage and took the key. He put it in the lock and turned it. The door opened. All four monkeys leapt out together.

"We are free!" cried the two little ones. "Where shall we go, Dad? Where shall we hide?"

"Don't get excited," said Muggle-Wump. "Calm down, everybody. Before we escape from this beastly place we have one very very important thing to do."

"What?" they asked him.

"We're going to turn those terrible Twits UPSIDE DOWN!"

"We're going to *what?*" they cried. "You must be joking, Dad!"

"I'm not joking," Muggle-Wump said. "We're going to turn both Mr. and Mrs. Twit UPSIDE DOWN with their legs in the air!"

"Don't be ridiculous," the Roly-Poly Bird said. "How can we possibly turn those two maggoty old monsters upside down?"

"We can, we can!" cried Muggle-Wump. "We are going to make them stand on their heads for hours and hours! Perhaps forever! Let *them* see what it feels like for a change!"

"How?" said the Roly-Poly Bird. "Just tell me how."

Muggle-Wump laid his head on one side and a tiny twinkling little smile touched the corners of his mouth. "Now and again," he said, "but not very often, I have a brilliant idea. This is one of them. Follow me, my friends, follow me." He scampered off toward the house and the three other monkeys and the Roly-Poly Bird went after him.

"Buckets and paintbrushes!" cried Muggle-Wump. "That's what we want next! There are plenty in the workshed! Hurry up, everyone! Get a bucket and a paintbrush!"

Inside Mr. Twit's workshed there was an enormous barrel of HUGTIGHT sticky glue, the stuff he used for catching birds. "Fill your buckets!" Muggle-Wump ordered. "We are now going into the big house!"

Mrs. Twit had hidden the key to the front door under the mat and Muggle-Wump had seen her doing it, so it was easy for them to get in. In they went, all four monkeys, with their buckets of sticky glue. Then came the Roly-Poly Bird flying in after them, with a bucket in his beak and a brush in his claw.

The Great Glue Painting Begins

"This is the living room," announced Muggle-Wump. "The grand and glorious living room where those two fearful frumptious freaks eat Bird Pie every week for supper!"

"Please don't mention Bird Pie again," said the Roly-Poly Bird. "It gives me the shudders."

"We mustn't waste time!" cried Muggle-Wump. "Hurry up, hurry up! Now the first thing is this! I want everyone to paint sticky glue all over the ceiling! Cover it all! Smear it in every corner!"

"Over the ceiling!" they cried. "Why the *ceiling?*"

"Never mind why!" shouted Muggle-Wump. "Just do as you're told and don't argue!"

"But how do we get *up* there?" they asked. "We can't reach."

"Monkeys can reach anywhere!" shouted Muggle-Wump. He was in a frenzy of excitement now, waving his paintbrush and his bucket and leaping about all over the room. "Come on, come on! Jump on the table! Stand on the chairs! Hop on each other's shoulders! Roly-Poly can do it flying! Don't stand there gaping! We have to hurry, don't you understand that? Those terrible Twits will be back any moment and this time they'll have *guns!* Get on with it, for heaven's sake! Get on with it!"

And so the great glue-painting of the ceiling began. All the other birds who had been sitting on the roof flew in to help, carrying paintbrushes in their claws and beaks. There were buzzards, wild ducks, woodpeckers, magpies, rooks, ravens and many more. Everyone was splashing away like mad and with so many helpers, the job was soon finished.

The Carpet Goes on the Ceiling

"What now?" they all said, looking at Muggle-Wump.

"Ah-ha!" cried Muggle-Wump. "Now for the fun! Now for the greatest upside-down trick of all time! Are you ready?"

"We're ready," said the monkeys. "We're ready," said the birds.

"Pull out the carpet!" shouted Muggle-Wump. "Pull this huge carpet out from under the furniture and stick it onto the ceiling!"

"Onto the *ceiling!*" cried one of the small monkeys. "But that's impossible, Dad!"

"I'll stick *you* onto the ceiling if you don't shut up!" snapped Muggle-Wump.

"He's dotty!" they cried.

"He's balmy!"

"He's batty!"

"He's nutty!"

"He's screwy!"

"He's wacky!" cried the Roly-Poly Bird. "Poor old Muggles has gone off his wump at last!"

"Oh, do stop shouting such rubbish and give me a hand," said Muggle-Wump, catching hold of one corner of the carpet. "Pull, you nitwits, pull!"

The carpet was enormous. It covered the entire floor from wall to wall. It had a red and gold pattern on it. It is not easy to pull an enormous carpet off the floor when the room is full of tables and chairs. "Pull!" yelled Muggle-Wump. "Pull, pull, pull!" He was like a demon hopping round the room and telling everyone what to do. But you couldn't blame him. After months and months of standing on his head with his family, he couldn't wait for the time when the terrible Twits would be doing the same thing. At least that's what he hoped.

With the monkeys and the birds all pulling and puffing, the carpet was dragged off the floor and finally hoisted up onto the ceiling. And there it stuck.

All at once, the whole ceiling of the living room was carpeted in red and gold.

The Furniture Goes Up

"Now the table, the big table!" shouted Muggle-Wump. "Turn the table upside down and put a dollop of sticky glue onto the bottom of each leg. Then we shall stick that onto the ceiling as well!"

Hoisting the huge table upside down onto the ceiling was not an easy job, but they managed it in the end.

"Will it stay there?" they cried. "Is the glue strong enough to hold it up?"

"It's the strongest glue in the world!" Muggle-Wump replied. "It's the special bird-catching bird-killing glue for smearing on trees!"

"Please," said the Roly-Poly Bird. "I have asked you before not to mention that subject. How would *you* like it if it was Monkey Pie they made every

Wednesday and all your friends had been boiled up and I went on talking about it?"

"I do beg your pardon," said Muggle-Wump. "I'm so excited I hardly know what I'm saying. Now the chairs! Do the same with the chairs! All the chairs must be stuck upside down to the ceiling! And in their right places! Oh, do hurry up, everybody! Any moment now, those two filthy freaks are going to come rushing in with their guns!"

The monkeys, with the birds helping them, put glue on the bottom of each chair leg and hoisted them up to the ceiling.

"Now the smaller tables!" shouted Muggle-Wump. "And the big sofa! And the sideboard! And the lamps! And all the tiny little things! The ashtrays! The ornaments! And that beastly plastic gnome on the sideboard! Everything, absolutely everything must be stuck to the ceiling!"

It was terribly hard work. It was especially difficult to stick everything onto the ceiling in exactly its right place. But they got it done in the end.

"What now?" asked the Roly-Poly Bird. He was out of breath and so tired he could hardly flap his wings.

"Now the pictures!" cried Muggle-Wump. "Turn all the pictures upside down! And will one of you birds please fly out onto the road and watch to see when those frumptious freaks are coming back."

"I'll go," said the Roly-Poly Bird. "I'll sit on the telephone wires and keep guard. It'll give me a rest."

The Ravens Swoop Over

They had only just finished the job when the Roly-Poly Bird came swooping in, screaming, "They're coming back! They're coming back!"

Quickly, the birds flew back onto the roof of the house. The monkeys rushed into their cage and stood upside down, one on top of the other. A moment later, Mr. and Mrs. Twit came marching into the garden, each carrying a fearsome-looking gun.

"I'm glad to see those monkeys are still upside down," said Mr. Twit.

"They're too stupid to do anything else," said Mrs. Twit. "Hey, look at all those cheeky birds still up there on the roof! Let's go inside and load our lovely new guns and then it'll be *bang bang bang* and Bird Pie for supper."

Just as Mr. and Mrs. Twit were about to enter the
house, two black ravens swooped low over their
heads. Each bird carried a paintbrush in its claw and
each paintbrush was smeared with sticky glue. As
the ravens whizzed over, they brushed a streak of
sticky glue onto the tops of Mr. and Mrs. Twit's
heads. They did it with the lightest touch but even
so the Twits both felt it.

"What was *that?*" cried Mrs. Twit. "Some beastly
bird has dropped his dirty droppings on my head!"

"On mine too!" shouted Mr. Twit. "I felt it! I felt
it!"

"Don't touch it!" cried Mrs. Twit. "You'll get it all
over your hands! Come inside and we'll wash it off
at the sink!"

"The filthy dirty brutes," yelled Mr. Twit. "I'll bet
they did it on purpose! Just wait till I've loaded up
my gun!"

Mrs. Twit got the key from under the doormat
(where Muggle-Wump had carefully replaced it) and
into the house they went.

The Twits Are Turned Upside Down

"*What's this?*" gasped Mr. Twit as they entered the living room.

"*What's happened?*" screamed Mrs. Twit.

They stood in the middle of the room, looking up. All the furniture, the big table, the chairs, the sofa,

the lamps, the little side tables, the cabinet with bottles of beer in it, the ornaments, the electric heater, the carpet, everything was stuck upside down to the ceiling. The pictures were upside down on the walls. And the floor they were standing on was absolutely bare. What's more, it had been painted white to look like the ceiling.

"*Look!*" screamed Mrs. Twit. "*That's the floor!
The floor's up there! This is the ceiling! We are
standing on the ceiling!*"

"We're UPSIDE DOWN!" gasped Mr. Twit. "We
must be upside down. We are standing on the ceiling
looking down at the floor!"

"Oh help!" screamed Mrs. Twit. "Help help help!
I'm beginning to feel giddy!"

"So am I! So am I!" cried Mr. Twit. "I don't like
this one little bit!"

"We're upside down and all the blood's going to
my head!" screamed Mrs. Twit. "If we don't do
something quickly, I shall die, I know I will!"

"I've got it!" cried Mr. Twit. "I know what we'll do! *We'll stand on our heads, then anyway we'll be the right way up!*"

So they stood on their heads, and of course, the moment the tops of their heads touched the floor, the sticky glue that the ravens had brushed on a few moments before did its job. They were stuck. They were pinned down, cemented, glued, fixed to the floorboards.

Through a crack in the door the monkeys watched. They'd jumped right out of their cage the moment the Twits had gone inside. And the Roly-Poly Bird watched. And all the other birds flew in and out to catch a glimpse of this extraordinary sight.

The Monkeys Escape

That evening, Muggle-Wump and his family went up to the big wood on top of the hill, and in the tallest tree of all they built a marvelous tree house. All the birds, especially the big ones, the crows and rooks and magpies, made their nests around the tree house so that nobody could see it from the ground.

"You can't stay up here forever, you know," the Roly-Poly Bird said.

"Why not?" asked Muggle-Wump. "It's a lovely place."

"Just you wait till the winter comes," the Roly-Poly Bird said. "Monkeys don't like cold weather, do they?"

"They most certainly don't!" cried Muggle-Wump. "Are the winters so very cold over here?"

"It's all snow and ice," said the Roly-Poly Bird. "Sometimes it's so cold a bird will wake up in the morning with his feet frozen to the bough that he's been roosting on."

"Then what shall we do?" cried Muggle-Wump. "My family will all be deep-freezed!"

"No, they won't," said the Roly-Poly Bird. "Because when the first leaves start falling from the trees in the autumn, you can all fly home to Africa with me."

"Don't be ridiculous," Muggle-Wump said. "Monkeys can't fly."

"You can sit on my back," said the Roly-Poly Bird. "I shall take you one at a time. You will travel by the Roly-Poly Super Jet and it won't cost you a penny!"

The Twits Get the Shrinks

And down here in the horrid house, Mr. and Mrs. Twit are still stuck upside down to the floor of the living room.

"It's all your fault!" yelled Mr. Twit, thrashing his legs in the air. "*You're* the one, you ugly old cow, who went hopping around shouting 'We're upside down! We're upside down!' "

"And *you're* the one who said to stand on our heads so we'd be the right way up, you whiskery old warthog!" screamed Mrs. Twit. "Now we'll never get free! We're stuck here forever!"

"*You* may be stuck here forever," said Mr. Twit. "But not me! I'm going to get away!"

Mr. Twit wriggled and squirmed, and he squiggled and wormed, and he twisted and turned, and he choggled and churned, but the sticky glue held him to the floor just as tightly as it had once held the poor birds in The Big Dead Tree. He was still as upside down as ever, standing on his head.

But heads are not made to be stood upon. If you stand on your head for a very long time, a horrid thing happens, and this was where Mr. Twit got his biggest shock of all. With so much weight on it from up above, his head began to get squashed into his body.

Quite soon, it had disappeared completely, sunk out of sight in the fatty folds of his flabby neck.

"I'm SHRINKING!" burbled Mr. Twit.

"So am I!" cried Mrs. Twit.

"Help me! Save me! Call a doctor!" yelled Mr. Twit. "I'm getting THE DREADED SHRINKS!"

And so he was. Mrs. Twit was getting THE DREADED SHRINKS, too! And this time it wasn't a fake. It was the real thing!

Their heads SHRANK into their necks . . .

Then their necks began SHRINKING into their bodies . . .

And their bodies began SHRINKING into their legs . . .

And their legs began SHRINKING into their feet . . .

And one week later, on a nice sunny afternoon, a man called Fred came round to read the gas meter. When nobody answered the door, Fred peeped into the house and there he saw, on the floor of the living room, two bundles of old clothes, two pairs of shoes, and a walking stick. There was nothing more left in this world of Mr. and Mrs. Twit.

And everyone, including Fred, shouted . . . "HOORAY!"

AN INTERVIEW WITH
Roald Dahl

This interview, conducted by family friend Todd McCormack, took place in 1988, when Roald Dahl was 71. As Dahl himself said, "I have worked all my life in a small hut up in our orchard. It is a quiet private place and no one has been permitted to pry in there." He not only let Todd McCormack inside the hut, but also gave him rare insight into how he worked, where his ideas came from, and how he shaped them into unforgettable stories. Roald Dahl passed away in 1990, two years after the interview.

What is it like writing a book?

When you're writing, it's rather like going on a very long walk, across valleys and mountains and things, and you get the first view of what you see and you write it down. Then you walk a bit further, maybe up onto the top of a hill, and you see something else. Then you write that and you go on like that, day after day, getting different views of the same landscape really. The highest mountain on the walk is obviously the end of the book, because it's got to be the best view of all, when everything comes together and you can look back and see that everything you've done all ties up. But it's a very, very long, slow process.

How do you get the ideas for your stories?

It starts always with a tiny little seed of an idea, a little germ, and that even doesn't come very easily. You can be mooching around for a year or so before you get a good one. When I do get a good one, mind you, I quickly write it down so that I won't forget it, because it disappears otherwise rather like a dream. But when I get it, I don't dash up here and start to write it. I'm very careful. I walk around it and look at it and sniff it and then see if I think it will go. Because once you start, you're embarked on a year's work and so it's a big decision.

How did you get the idea for James and the Giant Peach?

I had a kind of fascination with the thought that an apple—there're a lot of apple trees around here, and fruit trees, and you can watch them through the summer getting bigger and bigger from a tiny little apple to bigger and bigger ones, and it seemed to me an obvious thought—what would happen if it didn't stop growing? Why should it stop growing at a certain size? And this appealed to me and I thought this was quite a nice little idea and [then I had to think] of which fruit I should take for my story. I thought apple, pear, plum, peach. Peach is rather nice, a lovely fruit. It's pretty and it's big and it's squishy and you can go into it and it's got a big seed in the middle that you can play with. And so the story started.

What is your work routine?

My work routine is very simple and it's always been so for the last 45 years. The great thing, of course, is never to work too long at a stretch, because after about two hours you are not at your highest peak of concentration, so you have to stop. Some writers choose certain times to write, others [choose] other times, and it suits me to start rather late. I start at 10 o'clock and I stop at 12. Always. However well I'm going, I will stay there until 12, even if I'm a bit stuck. You have to keep your bottom on the chair and stick it out. Otherwise, if you start getting in the habit of walking away, you'll never get it done.

How do you keep the momentum going when you are writing a novel?

One of the vital things for a writer who's writing a book, which is a lengthy project and is going to take about a year, is how to keep the momentum going. It is the same with a young person writing an essay. They have got to write four or five or six pages. But when you are writing it for a year, you go away and you have to come back. I never come back to a blank page; I always finish about halfway through. To be confronted with a blank page is not very nice. But Hemingway, a great American writer, taught me the finest trick when you are doing a long book, which is, he simply said in his own words, "When you are going good, stop writing." And that means that if everything's going well and you know exactly where the end of the chapter's going to go and you know just what the people are going to do, you don't go on writing and writing until you come to the end of it, because when you do, then you say, well, where am I going to go next? And you get up and you walk away and you don't want to come back because you don't know where you want to go. But if you stop when you are going good, as Hemingway said…then you know what you are going to say next. You make yourself stop, put your pencil down and everything, and you walk away. And you can't wait to get back because you know what you want to say next and that's lovely and you have to try and do that. Every time, every day all the way through the year. If you stop when you are stuck, then you are in trouble!

WHAT IS THE SECRET TO KEEPING YOUR READERS ENTERTAINED?

My lucky thing is I laugh at exactly the same jokes that children laugh at and that's one reason I'm able to do it. I don't sit out here roaring with laughter, but you have wonderful inside jokes all the time and it's got to be exciting, it's got to be fast, it's got to have a good plot, but it's got to be funny. It's got to be funny. And each book I do is a different level of that. Oh, *The Witches* is quite different from *The BFG* or *James [and the Giant Peach]* or *Danny [the Champion of the World]*. The line between roaring with laughter and crying because it's a disaster is a very, very fine one. You see a chap slip on a banana skin in the street and you roar with laughter when he falls slap on his backside. If in doing so you suddenly see he's broken a leg, you very quickly stop laughing and it's not a joke anymore. I don't know, there's a fine line and you just have to try to find it.

HOW DO YOU CREATE INTERESTING CHARACTERS?

When you're writing a book, with people in it as opposed to animals, it is no good having people who are ordinary, because they are not going to interest your readers at all. Every writer in the world has to use the characters that have something interesting about them, and this is even more true in children's books. I find that the only way to make my characters *really* interesting to children is to exaggerate all their good or bad qualities, and so if a person is nasty or bad or cruel, you make them very nasty, very bad, very cruel. If they are ugly, you make them extremely ugly. That, I think, is fun and makes an impact.

HOW DO YOU INCLUDE HORRIFIC EVENTS WITHOUT SCARING YOUR READERS?

You never describe any horrors happening, you just say that they do happen. Children who got crunched up in Willy Wonka's chocolate machine were carried away and that was the end of it. When the parents screamed, "Where has he gone?" and Wonka said, "Well, he's gone to be made into fudge," that's where you laugh, because you don't see it happening, you don't hear the child screaming or anything like that ever, ever, ever.

HOW MUCH HAS LIVING IN THE COUNTRYSIDE INFLUENCED YOU?

I wouldn't live anywhere else except in the country, here. And, of course, if you live in the country, your work is bound to be influenced by it in a lot of ways, not pure fantasy like Charlie with chocolate factories, witches, and BFG's, but the others that are influenced by everything around you. I suppose the one [book] that is most dependent purely on this countryside around here is *Danny the Champion of the World,* and I rather love that book. And when I was planning it, wondering where I was going to let Danny and his father live, all I had to do, I didn't realize it, all I had to do was look around my own garden and there it was.

ROALD DAHL ON THE SUBJECT OF CHOCOLATE:

In . . . seven years of this glorious and golden decade [the 1930s], all the great classic chocolates were invented: the Crunchie, the Whole Nut bar, the Mars bar, the Black Magic assortment, Tiffin, Caramello, Aero, Malteser, the Quality Street assortment, Kit Kat, Rolo, and Smarties. In music the equivalent would be the golden age when compositions by Bach and Mozart and Beethoven were given to us. In painting it was the equivalent of the Renaissance in Italian art and the advent of the Impressionists toward the end of the nineteenth century. In literature it was Tolstoy and Balzac and Dickens. I tell you, there has been nothing like it in the history of chocolate and there never will be.

Roald Dahl, born in 1916 in
Wales, spent his childhood in England and later
worked in Africa. When World War II broke
out, he joined the Royal Air Force and became
a fighter pilot. After a war injury, he moved
to Washington, D.C., and there he began to
write. His first short story was published by
The Saturday Evening Post, and so began a long
and distinguished career.

Roald Dahl became, quite simply, one of
the best-loved children's book authors of all
time. Although he passed away in 1990, his
popularity and that of his many books—*Charlie
and the Chocolate Factory, James and the Giant Peach,
Danny the Champion of the World,* to name just a
few—continues to grow.

Visit www.roalddahl.com to learn more about
the author and his books.

※ ※ ※

Quentin Blake has
illustrated most of Roald Dahl's children's
books as well as many others. The first
Children's Laureate of the United Kingdom
and a recipient of the Kate Greenaway Medal,
Quentin Blake lives in London and teaches
illustration at the Royal College of Art.